Visions of
NEW ENGLAND
A State by State Pictorial Tour

CLB 1662
© 1986 Illustrations and text: Colour Library Books Ltd.,
    Guildford, Surrey, England.
Text filmsetting by Acesetters Ltd.. Richmond, Surrey, England.
Printed and bound in Barcelona. Spain by Cronion, S.A.
All rights reserved.
Published 1986 by DeWolfe & Fiske.
ISBN 0 517 623 82 X
h g f e d c b a
Dep. Leg. B-21.110-86

Visions of
NEW ENGLAND

A State by State Pictorial Tour

Text by
BILL HARRIS

DeWolfe & Fiske

Wherever and whenever beauty of landscape and shore is mentioned, New England must surely come to mind, and the picture most often imagined must just as surely be of this lovely region of America in the fall. Throughout the densely-forested states that make up New England: Maine, Vermont, New Hampshire, Massachusetts, Rhode Island and Connecticut, color fills the eye – vermilions, oranges, russets, greens and golds in every imaginable hue – all painted in broad strokes as far as the eye can see. Other seasons, too, have their charm. In winter the land rests under a blanket of crisp, white snow, taken advantage of by winter sports enthusiasts in their thousands who come to ski the slopes and skate the glassy, frozen lakes. Spring sees the blossoming of all manner and variety of flower, fruit and tree, and hot summer days, filled with sunshine, now tempt people onto the delightful Atlantic beaches, or into the splendor of the magnificent State Parks. But, for the real magic of New England, nothing can replace the sight or memory of those wonderful autumns.

New England still epitomizes rural America, with its white, wooden churches, red, clapboard houses (actually known as New England barn red, a color derived from the early settlers' use of ox-blood), gray, timbered barns, and the cranberries, maple syrup and succulent shellfish that are as much a part of the past as they are of the present. It is fitting, therefore, that it was here that the real story of America began, for New England's history goes back to 1620, when the Pilgrim Fathers arrived on the *Mayflower*, landed in what is present day Provincetown, and settled in Massachusetts. Their famous voyage was subsidized by a loan of £7,000, later redeemed by the sale of furs from Maine's beaver dams. After signing the Mayflower Compact they crossed the bay and founded the Plymouth Plantation. Soon, more Puritans arrived, seeking escape from religious persecution in England, and within four years 10,000 had settled. By the end of the century there were 80,000 – and 50,000 more had made their homes in Rhode Island, Connecticut and New Hampshire. With their religious zeal, their capacity for hard work, and their high standards, these early New Englanders forged a society of strong and independent people; people who contributed immeasurably to the making of America, for they and their descendants provided many of the nation's leaders, statesmen, writers and merchants and, in addition, they established many banking institutions and seats of learning.

Modern-day New England is a unique mix of the old and the new, the natural and the man-made. Bustling cities such as Boston and Hartford retain much of their old-world elegance and charm, and yet sacrifice none of their modern business efficiency. Major industries make use of the ingrained work ethic that has always marked the New Englander, while in her venerable colleges and universities New England offers the finest of educational facilities.

Despite all this, it is still back to those quiet, peaceful forests that the mind returns to savor the real spirit of this unique corner of America.

Facing page: White Mountain National Forest, New Hampshire.

CONNECTICUT

Nutmeg State

Population (1982): 3,153,000 (26th)

Size: 5,009 square miles (48th)

Entered Union: January 9, 1788 (5th)

State Motto: Qui Transtulit Sustinet (He Who is Transplanted Still Sustains)

State Flower: Mountain laurel

State Bird: Robin

State Tree: White oak

Industry: aircraft engines, submarines, helicopters, copper products, machine tools

Agriculture: tobacco, hay, apples, nursery stock

Anyone trying to convey a sense of small-town America can do it by calling the small town "Podunk." Though there is no such town, the name was given to a tribe of Indians living in the beautiful Connecticut River Valley in 1614 by the Dutch explorer Adriaen Block, the first European to visit there. By the time English settlers arrived from the Massachusetts colony 20 years later, the Dutch already had a tenuous claim on the place and an outpost of New Amsterdam on the site of what is now Hartford.

The tension between the two groups gave the American English language another pair of words. The Dutch were outnumbered and frightened to the point of building a wall at the north end of their colony, on Manhattan Island, to keep the English out. The site is known everywhere in the world today as Wall Street. But wall or no, the Dutch knew in their hearts that it was only a matter of time before their Connecticut neighbors would overrun them and they covered their fears with a bravado that, to them at least, passed for wit. The English were known as "John Bull" even then, and Peter Stuyvesant's followers thought it was great fun to mock them as "John Cheese" whenever they had an encounter. In their language, John Cheese is "Jon Quese," which to British ears came out as "Yankee," a word Connecticut people used all over New England to describe themselves.

Nearness to New York has always loomed large in the development of Connecticut. Though never really great farming country, the hills and valleys, the northern coast of Long Island Sound, are strikingly beautiful and almost from the beginning wealthy New Yorkers were lured there in search of a house in the country.

The result, in part at least, is that though Connecticut is one of the smallest of the states, its per-capita income is one of the highest. It has become corporate headquarters to some of America's biggest companies, too, and its rolling hills are as much dotted with stainless steel and glass as with the quaint stone walls that have been a Connecticut institution since the earliest days.

After Yale University settled down in New Haven in 1716, the state became a haven for education and Connecticut is home to many of the best prep schools in the country, where future Ivy Leaguers get a head start not only on their education, but on their social contacts as well.

Before the Revolution, England's government placed restrictions on the amount of manufacturing that could be done in Connecticut. The Connecticut Yankees got even during the war, when they became the new country's biggest producer of arms and ammunition. Samuel Colt, inventor of the "gun that won the West," started his career in Hartford; the Winchester company in New Haven provided the long rifles. And that may be one reason why Hartford has been America's insurance capital for generations.

Facing page: Yale University, New Haven, Connecticut.

Covered bridges, such as the one at West Cornwall (right), are a familiar sight in Connecticut's charming, unspoilt countryside (this page), as are the many quaint little villages with their white clapboard houses and colonial churches. Facing page: (top left) Windsor, (center left) Riverton, (bottom left) a church in Winchester, (bottom right) farmland near Litchfield, with its Town Hall (bottom center) and the lovely Congregational Church (top right) on Litchfield Green.

Hartford (previous pages) is the capital of Connecticut and contains many buildings of great elegance and grandeur, including (left) the cathedral and (right) the Capitol. The coast of Connecticut offers a variety of pastimes, from swimming at the fine beaches of Rocky Neck State Park (this page) to experiencing the past at Mystic Seaport (facing page), a "living" museum with an impressive display of 19th-century ships and buildings.

When Mystic (these and previous pages) was first settled its inhabitants
looked to the sea for their livelihood, and by the mid-19th century
fishing, whaling and shipbuilding had become flourishing industries. Today,
the atmosphere of this maritime lifestyle can still be experienced, with
the re-enactment of old crafts and pastimes against a background of
historic buildings and beautifully-preserved vessels.

Connecticut has many beautiful parks, including (right) Wadsworth Falls State Park and (facing page) Harkness Memorial State Park, which was once the private estate of the Harkness family. The main feature of Devils Hopyard State Park (above) is the Chapman Falls. Allegedly, the potholes at the base of the falls were made by the Devil as he hopped from ledge to ledge keeping out of the water. Top: Bashan Falls, near Moodus.

RHODE ISLAND

Ocean State

Population (1982): 958,000 (41st)

Size: 1,214 square miles (50th)

Entered Union: May 29, 1790 (13th)

State Motto: Hope

State Flower: Violet

State Bird: Rhode Island red

State Tree: Red maple

Industry: jewelry, machinery, textiles, electronics

Agriculture: potatoes, apples, corn

There are so many farms and forests, wetlands and bays in Rhode Island, it's hard to believe that it is the smallest of the 50 states. Though it is only 48 miles from the northern to the southern tip, it has 76 miles of Atlantic Ocean shoreline and 170 miles of coastline on its inland waters. Narragansett Bay, extending from Newport to Providence, is bordered by hills and pastureland and dotted with small, peaceful towns. The overall effect is that there is plenty of room to spread out in Rhode Island.

It all began in 1636, when a clergyman named Roger Williams had a falling out with the Massachusetts Puritans and moved down to the head of Narragansett Bay to found a more liberal colony at Providence. Within ten years, others had followed him and there were thriving towns at Newport, Warwick and Portsmouth, too. They eventually banded together and Williams secured a Royal charter to make it all legal. The city of Newport had been settled by John Clarke and William Coddington, who had been banished from Massachusetts for their liberal tendencies regarding religion. They bought an island in the Bay that the Indians who sold it to them had called Aquidneck. Before long they changed its name to the "Isle of Rhodes," which later became the basis for the name of the whole state. The suggestion had come as far back as 1524, when the explorer Verrazano landed on Block Island and noted in his log that it reminded him of the Mediterranean island of Rhodes.

The lure of true religious freedom brought hundreds to the new colony and Rhode Island quickly shifted from farming to ship building and seafaring. In the years before the Revolutionary War, Newport was the center of the slave trade and in the process became one of the wealthiest cities in America. In spite of it, the state outlawed slaves in 1774, almost 35 years before the rest of the country followed suit.

Privateers took up the slack and made Newport wealthier still, and by the 1760s it was the resort of choice for plantation owners from the South and from the West Indies who went north to escape the heat of the summer. Even though the city went into decline as a major port after the Revolution, the tourist wave continued and after the Civil War, Ward McAllister, a former Southerner who had known Newport as a youngster, set himself up as the organizer of New York society and lured the likes of the Astors and Belmonts to the city at the end of Narragansett Bay.

The houses they built to demonstrate their wealth are what lure tourists there today, but the real lure is what it has always been, a unique combination of wild seascapes and peaceful landscapes.

Facing page: Newport Bridge, Newport, Rhode Island.

Providence, Rhode Island's capital city, boasts one of America's most magnificent capitols (facing page). Made of white Georgia marble, it is crowned by the world's second largest unsupported marble dome, topped by a symbolic bronze figure, *The Independant Man*. At the turn of the century Newport was a millionaires' playground dotted with lavish private mansions, such as those on Ocean Drive at Brenton Point (above), many of which are now museums. Apart from these palaces, the city contains many smaller, yet equally attractive colonial-style homes and some interesting public buildings (overleaf pages).

Much of Newport's appeal lies in its variety and contrast. The town contains both quiet, cobbled streets, including Thames Street (above), as well as luxury residential areas such as the famous Bellevue Avenue, on which is situated Marble House (facing page). Different types of marble from around the world have been used in the design of this sumptuous mansion, which was built in 1892 for William K. Vanderbilt and modeled on the 17th and 18th-century architecture of Versailles. Overleaf pages: Newport Bridge stretches gracefully across Narragansett Bay.

MASSACHUSETTS

Bay State

Population (1982): 5,781,000 (11th)

Size: 8,257 square miles (45th)

Entered Union: February 6, 1788 (6th)

State Motto: Ense Petit Placidam Sub Libertate Quietem (By The Sword We Seek
Peace, But Only Peace Under Liberty)

State Flower: Mayflower

State Bird: Chickadee

State Tree: American elm

Industry: electronics, printing, instruments, machinery

Agriculture: nursery products, apples, corn, tobacco

At least once a year, on Thanksgiving Day, all America is reminded of what we like to call "the Pilgrim Fathers," the people who established the first colony at Plymouth in Massachusetts. In a country without an established aristocracy, generations tried to establish themselves as descendants of the passengers of the Mayflower and, thus, more American than most.

The Pilgrims actually had set sail for Virginia, or at least they said that's where they were going, and claimed to have landed in the wrong place. By having done so, they were free to be independent of the British company that owned Virginia and completely independent of England herself. The rest, as they say, is history.

The history of the United States is preserved in Massachusetts more than anywhere else, especially in the Boston area where the American Revolution began, where the first great stirrings of the Abolitionist movement that led to the Civil War led to lynchings and fiery oratory, where the country's first literary and educational successes let the world know that this was no nation of country bumpkins.

Massachusetts is the state that produced the Adams family and the Kennedy family; it was where the Cabots and the Lowells put an American stamp on the Industrial Revolution. It's the home of Harvard and Amherst and MIT, more universities, in fact than almost

any other state. Lexington and Concord, where the War for Independence began, is home today for people who work in one of the world's biggest concentrations of research and electronics facilities.

It's the home of the Boston Symphony and the Boston Pops, of the Berkshire Mountains and hundreds of miles of beautiful beaches. It's quaint little towns and bustling, growing cities. It's Cape Cod and Nantucket and Martha's Vineyard.

For all its rich history, Massachusetts seems right now to be at the peak of its greatness. Though they claimed to be here for religious reasons, the Puritans who established the Massachusetts Bay Colony were hard-headed businessmen and from the very first, their official policies were more oriented toward profit than Puritanism. But religion was important, of course, and when waves of Irish Catholics began arriving after 1845, differences in religion were too important. The old Yankees exploited the newcomers and the newcomers exploited each other.

It is all past history now. Rivalry between ethnic groups has lessened, and though the Massachusetts tradition of individualism is as strong as it ever was, there is more togetherness there now than ever before. And though they like living in small towns and in small houses, the tradition is to think big. And to think young.

Facing page: the gold-domed State Capitol, Boston.

Previous pages: aerial views of Boston, showing (left) Long Wharf with the distinctive Custom House Tower and (right) the soaring towers of the Prudential Center and, in the right foreground, the domed, Renaissance-style church of the Christian Science Center, shown in more detail (facing page). This page: apart from its larger, more impressive buildings, Boston has preserved much of the charming, homely architecture of former days. With brownstone houses lining cobbled, gas-lit streets, Beacon Hill (top right and bottom pictures), located on the northern side of Boston Common, is the city's oldest residential area. Top left: Copp's Hill Burial Ground, one of the city's oldest cemeteries. In the 1800s, the summits of both Copp's Hill and Beacon Hill were leveled to provide earth for enlarging the Boston Peninsula. Top center: Old West Church.

34

Previous pages: (right) the Charles River, spanned by Weeks Memorial Foot Bridge, and in the foreground, part of Harvard University, and (left) the impressive buildings of Massachusetts Institute of Technology. These two famous universities are both situated in Cambridge, which was originally settled by farmers in 1630 under the name of New Towne. The area is joined to Boston's Beacon Hill by Longfellow Bridge (above), named after the 19th-century poet Henry Wadsworth Longfellow, who studied at Harvard alongside many great artists and thinkers. Facing page: moored at Griffith's Wharf is a replica of the brig *Beaver II*.

42

Previous pages: (left) an aerial view of central Boston dominated by the white spire of Old North Church, and (right) snow-covered Boston Common, with the the State Capitol's gilded dome gleaming through bare, winter trees. Now laced by a network of paths and footways, the common (above) was originally a cow pasture and is America's oldest public park. The First Church of the Christian Science Center (facing page), which is the world headquarters of the Christian Science faith, was built in 1894 and the impressive domed extension added in 1904.

Much of Boston's finest architecture is to be found in Copley Square, in the city's Back Bay area (previous pages left). As well as fine neo-Romanesque buildings, such as Trinity Church (facing page, top right), the square boasts some striking modern structures, including the John Hancock Tower, with its mirrored-glass exterior shown (previous page right) throwing a reflection of golden sunlight across the Charles River. The Public Gardens (facing page, remaining pictures) are famed for their lovely flowers, specimen trees and fine statuary, which includes the equestrian statue of George Washington (bottom right). In the summer, swan boat rides (above) can be taken on the park's lagoon.

The Charles River (facing page) sweeps gracefully through Boston. Inland from the city is Concord, where the American War of Independence began in April 1775. The town contains many historic attractions, including (left) the Minuteman statue, (bottom left) the Old Manse, and (below) Minuteman National Historical Park. Bottom: Wachusett Mountain.

Pliny Freeman Farm (facing page) is part of Old Sturbridge Village, where the rural lifestyle of the early 1800s has been vividly recalled. Another of New England's restored areas is Deerfield, which displays many of its original buildings, such as the beautifully restored Sheldon-Hawks House (above). The village has a fascinating and tragic history. In 1672 all 125 inhabitants were either killed or driven away by the Pocumtuck Indians in the Bloody Brook Massacre. By 1686 the village had been resettled, but after eight years the Indians struck again, killing 50 villagers, enslaving 100 and burning down half the buildings.

5

One of the many charms of New England is the way the landscape changes so dramatically from one season to another. At Deerfield (above) autumn's warm colors carpet the ground and almost hide an old clapboard house, while along the coast south of Boston, at Duxbury (facing page), a seascape is transformed by winter's harsh, white snow and cold blue sky.

The town of Plymouth was one of the first English-speaking settlements in America and has many historic attractions, including the Jenney Grist Mill (top left) and Pilgrim Village (above, left and top), which recreates the Plymouth of 1627. Facing page: the First Congregational Church at Williams College, around which the lovely settlement of Williamstown developed.

Previous pages left: the Highland Light of 1797, the oldest lighthouse on Cape Cod. Previous pages right: the granite canopy of the Plymouth Rock Memorial protects the rock on which the Pilgrims reputedly first landed at Plymouth in 1620. However, before crossing Cape Cod Bay to alight on the famous rock, the weary travelers first disembarked from the *Mayflower* at Provincetown (above), on the tip of Cape Cod's hook. The 252-foot tower of the Pilgrim Memorial honors this historic landing and is shown (facing page) dominating the town's skyline.

As suggested by its lively harbor (previous pages), Provincetown's main industry is, and has long been, fishing. Situated at the anchor end of the great, graceful curve of Cape Cod's National Seashore is beautiful Nauset Beach (these pages). This lonely stretch of golden sand is among the finest beaches on the east coast and boasts Nauset Beach Light (above), one of the area's many historic old lighthouses. Overleaf: (right) Dennis, one of the centers of the Cape's famous cranberry growing areas, and (left) the harbor of Menemsha, a picturesque fishing village on the lovely summer resort island of Martha's Vineyard.

From the air, the blue and emerald sea off the coast of Cape Cod can resemble some vast, tranquil lake. Yet often the seascape is wild and dramatic as Atlantic waves, whipped by fierce northeast winds, crash onto the unprotected eastern shores, each year claiming a little more of the land. Katama Bay (facing page) and Chappaquiddick Island (overleaf left) are both off the coast of Martha's Vineyard. Moored at Plymouth's State Pier (overleaf right) is a replica of the Pilgrims' vessel, *the Mayflower II.*

VERMONT

Green Mountain State

Population (1982): 516,000 (48th)

Size: 9,609 square miles (43rd)

Entered Union: March 4, 1791 (14th)

State Motto: Freedom and Unity

State Flower: Red clover

State Bird: Hermit thrush

State Tree: Sugar maple

Industry: tools, furniture, skis, fishing equipment, computer products

Agriculture: apples, maple sugar, corn, dairy products

One of the toughest trivia questions about the 50 states would be one that asks for the name of the one with the highest rural population. Almost nobody would guess it was Vermont, 66 percent of whose citizens live in rural settings. And it has the country's toughest land use laws that severely restrict ski resorts and shopping malls. Yet it is the 18th most industrialized state.

It is also considered to be one of the most typically "New England" of the New England States, and that makes it all the more attractive to visitors and newcomers. "The qualities of Vermont that were once considered backward are now in vogue," says a state official. "The only reason we have all these lovely old buildings and churches is that nobody had the money to tear them down." "But," adds another, "newcomers pay us the ultimate compliment by trying to imitate us."

It may be that per capita income is lower than in 37 other states, but people migrating there seem to feel that the quality of life in Vermont is a fair tradeoff.

It's a quality of life that hasn't changed much since Colonial times. It has made a typical Vermonter self-reliant, stubborn, independent. They are tolerant and slow to anger, except if someone tries to tell them how to live their lives. And above all, they share a great love for the State of Vermont.

Who can blame them? It's a beautiful place. The three ranges of the Green Mountains come by their name honestly, except in the fall, when their brilliant colors put even the Grand Canyon to shame. There is hardly a barren spot anywhere among its peaks or its notches. The Taconic Mountains along the New York border are gently-rounded and inviting, and form the western boundary of the beautiful Valley of Vermont which merges in the north with the rolling meadows toward the 107-mile-long Lake Champlain. There are more than 400 lakes and ponds in Vermont, and any competition to name the most beautiful of them would surely end up with a hung jury.

Interspersed among it all, the hand of man has created graceful, spired churches and tree-shaded village commons. The countryside is dotted with red barns and pretty white farmhouses, with neatly furrowed fields and peaceful pastures. It has covered bridges and general stores, quaint old inns and a general feeling of travelling back in time to better days.

In spite of an old Vermonter's statement that "A Vermont year is nine months winter and three months of damn poor sleddin'," the climate in Vermont is as delightful as the countryside, though it does get cold in winter, to the delight of skiers up in Killington, Woodstock and other slopes that make it the biggest skiing state east of the Rockies.

Facing page: the fabulous colors of fall in Vermont.

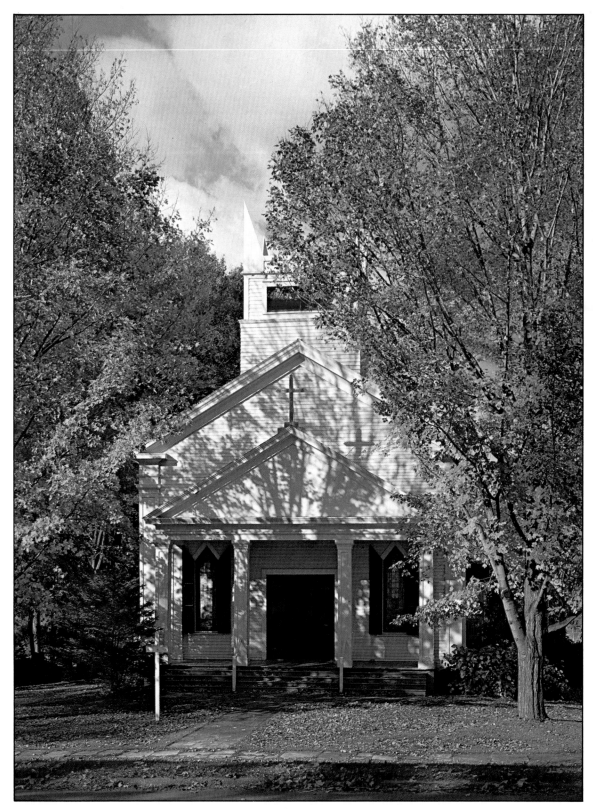

This page: some of the charming, white colonial-style buildings in the town of Manchester. Vermont is famed for its maple syrup, which is extracted from the tree's sap in wooden sugarhouses (facing page). Overleaf: the ski resort of Killington (left) and the frozen lake (right) are both near Rutland.

Before the harsh mid-winter sets in to whiten Vermont's hills and woodlands (previous pages), gentle early snowfalls serve to highlight the few remaining colors of fall. The state's capital, Montpelier (these pages) is situated in the lovely green valley of the Winooski River. The city has a vibrant cultural life, with concerts and festivals held throughout the year. It also boasts many fine old houses and a splendid State Capitol (above) with its gilded dome topped by a statue of Ceres, goddess of agriculture.

Few can fail to be moved by the magnificence of Vermont in the fall, when nature paints the trees with fiery reds and glowing oranges (previous pages left). Although Rutland is the state's second largest city and a busy industrial center, it is surrounded by beautiful and fertile land, which supports a number of farms (previous pages right) typical of New England. Bordered by the Taconic Mountain Range to the west and the Green Mountains to the east, this area also has a wealth of small rivers and streams (facing page) which babble excitedly when the last snows of winter begin to melt. Above: towards the end of summer, vivid autumn colors can be seen bursting through dense, green foliage. Overleaf: (left) a dreamlike scene of the Winooski River at Waterbury and (right) horses grazing at the village of Peru.

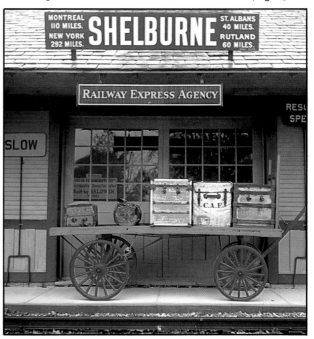

Previous pages left: horses in Peru. Thunderous clouds loom over a lonely farm (previous pages right) and a cemetery (facing page). Historic buildings and lush farmland contribute to the charm of Shelburne (this page). Overleaf: (left) countryside near the town of Morrisville (right).

NEW HAMPSHIRE

Granite State

Population (1982): 951,000 (42nd)

Size: 9,304 square miles (44th)

Entered Union: June 21, 1788 (9th)

State Motto: Live Free or Die

State Flower: Lilac

State Bird: Purple finch

State Tree: Birch

Industry: leather products, wood products, electrical equipment, machinery

Agriculture: apples, dairy products, vegetables

Though regarded by many as typically bucolic New England, New Hampshire has the fourth-largest proportion of factory workers in the country. It is also the fastest-growing state, except for Florida, east of the Mississippi River. Particularly in the south, it is a land of garish shopping malls, high technology industrial plants and condominium developments that are squeezing out some of its quaint New England-style towns.

It is conservative politically, with the result that it is, along with Alaska, unique among the 50 states in not having either a sales tax or an income tax. It is also in the bottom ten in spending for education, for prisons or for welfare.

The philosophy is that the towns, and not the state, and certainly not the Federal Government, should take care of such things. It has been a New Hampshire article of faith since Colonial times. At the begining of the Revolutionary War, it found itself the only New England state still loyal to the Crown and the only one run directly from England. By the end of the War, when there was no more British authority in this part of North America, New Hampshire still hadn't organized its own government. In the confusion, the towns took over and became so powerful in state affairs that, when a legislature was formed, it was organized to include one member for each town regardless of its size. They still operate in New Hampshire that way today and it has the third-largest legislative body in the English speaking world. The other two are the United States Congress and the British House of Commons.

But if its government is peculiar compared to most other states, it was not for nothing that the poet Robert Frost once said "It is restful just to think about New Hampshire." It is a place of fast-moving rivers and deep forests, of majestic granite mountains and restful lakes surrounded by fragrant pines. It is the home state of Daniel Webster, one of the most respected United States Senators in the history of the country, ironically elected by the people of Massachusetts, his adopted state.

Many Americans get an intimate look at New Hampshire every four years when the race for the Presidency begins there in early March. Though the media swears it isn't all that important, that doesn't stop them from braving the cold to troop around the Granite State testing the icy waters to find out who's going to be eliminated from the race in the first Presidential Primary of the year. It all began with the first primaries established right before the First World War. New Hampshire set an early date to beat the spring thaw and its inevitable mud. Over the years, other states have changed their laws to make them first, but the New Hampshire Legislature is always ready to move the date back further if necessary. After all, it's a boost to the economy and outsiders do contribute mightily to the cost of running New Hampshire.

Facing page: a forest home at Jackson, New Hampshire.

Mount Washington Hotel (these pages), the centerpiece of the Bretton Woods resort, boasts a fabulous location, being situated at the foot of the Presidential Range in the White Mountains region. The hotel is New England's largest frame structure and dates from the early days of this century, when guests would travel there in their own private locomotives or in one of the fifty public trains that would arrive each day during the warmer months.

Mount Washington's peak rises to 6,288 feet, and when a cog railroad to the summit was considered in the mid-1800s some thought the idea tantamount to building "a railroad to the moon." However, in the spring of 1866 work began on what was to be the world's first mountain-climbing cog railway, and by July 4 1869, it was successfully completed and ready to take passengers. This engineering marvel is still functioning today and uses three and a half miles of trestle-mounted track to climb the mountain's formidable slopes, reaching its terminus (above) one hour later. Facing page: mist rolls into the Washington Valley.

The Middle Kinsman Falls (above left), a stream leading to The Pool (facing page) and The Flume (above right), an impressive 800-foot gorge, are some of the breathtaking sights in Franconia Notch, a deep, 6,500-acre valley between the Franconia and Kinsman Mountain ranges. This area is part of New Hampshire's most magnificent scenery and as a summer resort has attracted such notable visitors as Nathaniel Hawthorne, Washington Irving and Henry Wadsworth Longfellow. Also a major ski center, Franconia possesses the country's first aerial tramway, which was built in 1938 and still ascends Cannon Mountain, giving splendid views of the Notch.

From a lookout point on Sugar Hill (above) Franconia's great natural beauty unfolds, and in the fall this can be particularly dazzling as an array of rich colors reaches out toward the horizon. Apart from its scenic attraction, Sugar Hill is well known as the site of the country's first ski school, Peckett's-on-Sugar-Hill. Founded in 1929, the school has long since gone although the skiing continues. A stream in Franconia Notch (facing page) tumbles over its granite bed, which has been rendered smooth by centuries of incessant wearing.

Amid the rugged beauty of the White Mountains there is much to see, including (above) the dense woodland and (top) secluded falls in Pinkham Notch, (left) the Episcopal Church of St. Matthew at Sugar Hill, and (facing page) the Saco River winding through Crawford Notch.

North Conway (these pages) is the southeastern gateway to the White Mountains and offers superb views of the snow-capped peaks. It is a busy tourist center equipped with many hotels, motels and restaurants, as well as attractions such as the Conway Scenic Railroad, which takes passengers along the Saco River in charming little steam locomotives (facing page). The railway's depot also contains a modest but interesting train museum.

Typical of a New England state, New Hampshire's scenery assumes a magical beauty during the fall (these pages). Leaves of russet and gold are contrasted by the blue of distant hills and sparkling streams, or reflected in smooth waters, such as those of the vast and lovely Lake Winnipesaukee (right), which covers 72 square miles.

Tufton Corner (left), characteristic of many New Hampshire towns, has strong links with the values and customs of the past. Here a traditional form of democracy exists, where the citizens hold regular meetings and all participate in the town's decision making. Below left: the red exterior of an old farm building stands out against the rugged countryside. Below: the White Mountains assume a blend of subtle colors as they stretch over the land as far as the eye can see. Facing page: a covered bridge over the Beebe River at Blair. These bridges are often quaintly known as "kissing" bridges.

MAINE

Pine Tree State

Population (1982): 1,133,000 (38th)

Size: 33,215 square miles (39th)

Entered Union: March 15, 1820 (23rd)

State Motto: Dirigo (I Direct)

State Flower: White pine cone

State Bird: Chickadee

State Tree: White pine

Industry: paper and wood products, textiles, leather, processed food

Agriculture: potatoes, apples, vegetables

If you were to take a helicopter ride along the Maine coast north from the New Hampshire border to Nova Scotia, you'd travel about 225 miles. If it were possible to walk the coast between the same two points, the distance would be more than 3500 miles. New York and Los Angeles are only 2800 miles apart, and the terrain is an easier hike. There are also more than 200 offshore islands on the Maine coast, adding hundreds more miles to what many regard as the most beautiful seacoast in the world.

But if Maine is linked to the sea, there is more to it that would make it a beautiful place even without the drama of the surf pounding on granite and the spectacular storms the people there call "goose-drownders." It's a place of lush, quiet forests, with meadows carpeted with wildflowers, and sparkling blue lakes. It's dotted with tidy little towns and cities that do all they can to keep their small-town charm.

More than half of the State of Maine is wild and untouched, partly because until very recent times it was inaccessible, but mostly because of the character of the people who call the State of Maine their home.

They prefer to be called "Down-Easters," even though the finger of land they live on is clearly "up" from the rest of the continental United States. It's a term that goes back to the days when Maine was officially part of Massachusetts and the only way to get there was by sailing down the prevailing west wind.

It never was easy to get there, which may help to explain why a real Down-Easter isn't quite like other Americans. They have a reputation for being close-mouthed, for instance, and when they do speak it's in accents not quite like any other. They enjoy a good story, but most sincerely believe in the old axiom: "Laugh before breakfast, weep before supper." But if that implies they are humorless and unfriendly, the picture is not quite accurate. They are probably more like the original New Englanders than anyone living in the New England states today. They believe in thrift and hard work, they are proud of their native horse sense and their ability to survive harsh winters without resorting to the trappings of the 20th century. They believe that cleanliness is next to Godliness, and that Godliness is the most important of mankind's aspirations.

They live closer to nature than most Americans, and they live more by the values we associate with the American pioneers than anybody, including Alaskans.

They have a fierce loyalty to their state, and refer to all other Americans as "Out-of-Staters." It's not that they don't like the rest of us, but they know they have something special that the rest of us will never quite feel no matter how hard we try.

Facing page: sunrise from the top of Mount Cadillac, Maine.

Previous pages left: lobster pots on a pier at Beals Island. The coast of New England is famed for its old lighthouses and those in Maine that are still operated by keepers have retained a timeless sense of romance. Despite the immaculate look of its striking exterior, West Quoddy Head Lighthouse (previous pages right) dates from 1807, and stands on the easternmost point of the United States mainland. It is called "West" as it lies west of East Quoddy Head in Canada. Bass Harbor Light (facing page) on Mount Desert Island, was built in 1858 and is one of Maine's loveliest lights as it sits on ruggedly beautiful rocks at the mouth of Bass Harbor. Above: Newagen seen from the Boothbays.

Since the mid-1800s Mount Desert Island has attracted vacationers with its breathtaking scenery. Today, visitors generally frequent the island's eastern side, while in the west a quiet, gentle lifestyle rolls on, relatively unspoilt by tourism. Southwest Harbor (previous pages left) is one of the secluded western villages where fishing and boat building are the major activities. Seal Harbor (previous pages right), on the eastern peninsula, is a popular yachting resort which comes alive during the summer with regattas, races and cruises. Away from the coast, tranquil blue lakes and dense forests (above) contribute to the island's natural beauty, much of which falls within the 33,000-acre Acadia National Park (facing page). Overleaf: (left) the handsome State House, Augusta, which was built by Charles Bulfinch between 1829 and 1832, and (right) Port Clyde, a small fishing town southwest of Mount Desert Island.

The sleepy little town of Wiscasset (previous pages left) seems far removed from its lively past as the busiest port north of Boston. Previous pages right: lobster floats at an old house in Owl's Head. Left and bottom right: houses on Orrs Island, (bottom left) South Freeport and (below) an enticing beach near Yarmouth. Facing page: (top center) Southport, (remaining pictures) Boothbay Harbor, a popular summer resort.

Cape Elizabeth Lighthouse (right), built in 1829, has the most powerful beam to shine from New England's coast, being visible up to 27 miles away. Maine's oldest lighthouse is Portland Head (bottom left and facing page), which was built in 1791 amid some of the state's most spectacular coastal scenery. Below and bottom right: Biddeford Pool.

INDEX